QED Everybody Feels...

Scared

Jane Bingham

QED Publishing

QED

A Catalogue record for this book is
available from the British Library.

ISBN 1 84538 391 5

Written by Jane Bingham
Designed by Alix Wood
Editor Clare Weaver
Illustrations Helen Turner

Publisher Steve Evans
Editorial Director Jean Coppendale
Art Director Zeta Davies

Printed and bound in China

Contents

Feeling scared

People have lots of different **feelings**.

They can feel happy.

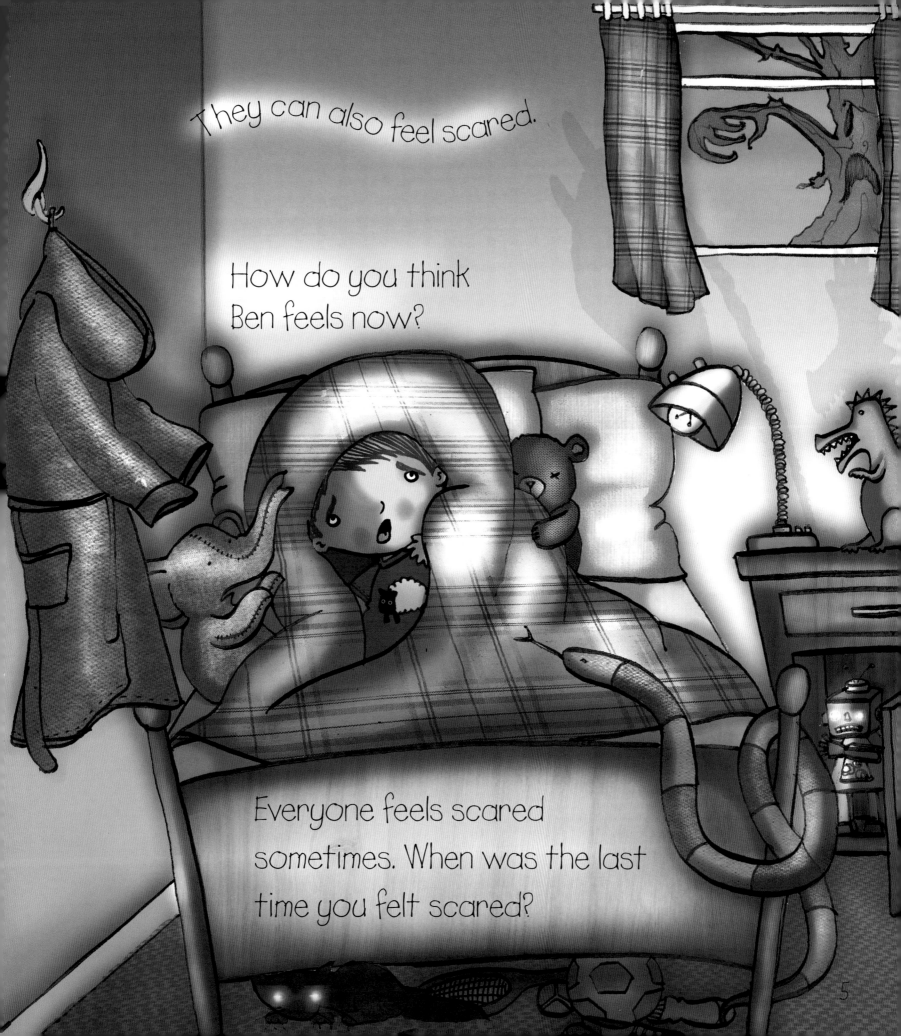

They can also feel scared.

How do you think Ben feels now?

Everyone feels scared sometimes. When was the last time you felt scared?

How does it feel?

If you are scared, you may feel **shaky**.
Your heart may beat very fast.

You may want to run away as fast as you can.
Or you may just want to curl up and hide.

Nobody likes feeling scared.

But **usually** this feeling doesn't last for long.

What makes you scared?

All sorts of things make people feel scared.

Here's what happened to Maya and Jack.

Maya's story

My name is Maya. The day I started school, I felt really scared.

I didn't have any **friends** at school.

I didn't know what I was meant to do.

I just wanted to go home!

When Mum said goodbye, I started to cry.

But my teacher told me not to be scared.

She was very **kind** to me.

Then we did some painting.

The teacher really liked my picture.

So did everyone!

At **playtime**, I made lots of friends.

Can Jack come home with me?

I wasn't scared of school any more.

Jack's story

I'm Jack. One day, I went shopping with Dad.

I saw a brilliant **model** castle.

The castle was great, but where was Dad?

I looked everywhere, but he had **vanished**.

I felt icy cold all over.

I thought I was
lost **forever**.

Dad and I **hugged** each other for a long time.

Then we all had tea together.

Don't be scared

If you see someone who looks scared,
try to **comfort** them.

It will make them feel much better!

Don't be scared.

21

Glossary

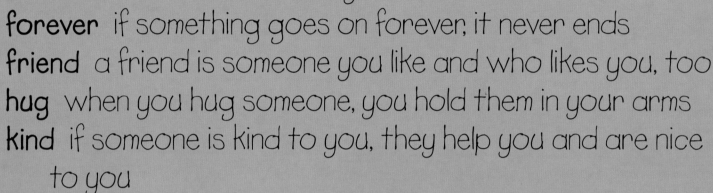

comfort when you comfort someone, you are
   kind to them and make them feel better

feelings your feelings tell you how you are
   and what kind of mood you're in

forever if something goes on forever, it never ends

friend a friend is someone you like and who likes you, too

hug when you hug someone, you hold them in your arms

kind if someone is kind to you, they help you and are nice
   to you

model castle a model castle is a small copy of a castle that
   you can put together yourself and use for playing games

playtime at playtime, all the children in a school stop their
   lessons and play with their friends

shaky if you're feeling shaky, you don't feel very strong and
   sometimes you can't stop your arms or legs from
   wobbling

usually if something usually happens, it nearly always
   happens

vanish if someone vanishes, they disappear suddenly and
   you can't see them

Index

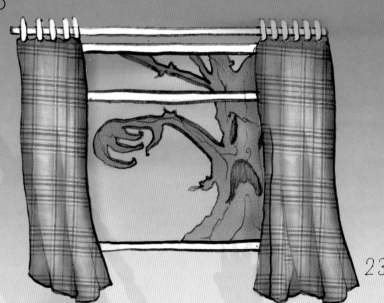

23

Notes for parents and teachers

- Look at the front cover of the book together. Talk about the picture. Can your children guess what the book is going to be about? Read the title together.

- Read the first line on page 4: 'People have lots of different feelings.' Help your children to make a list of different feelings.

- Ask your children to draw some simple faces showing different feelings. Then talk about them. Which feelings make your children feel good? Which don't feel so good?

- Talk about what happens to Ben on pages 4–5. Discuss Ben's feelings – first, when his bedroom light is on, and then when the light is switched off. Does Ben feel different?

- Ask your children how they feel about being in the dark. Does it sometimes make them scared? Explain that it's quite normal to be scared of the dark, but really there's nothing to be frightened of.

- Read the question on page 5: 'When was the last time you felt scared?' Talk with your children about the times when they have been scared.

- Read about how it feels to be scared (pages 6–7). Ask your children how they feel when they are scared.

- Read page 8 together, and look at the picture of Ben feeling better. Ask your children how they think Ben feels now. What do they think Ben's dad said to him?

- Look at the first part of Maya's story together (pages 10–11). Ask your children how they think Maya feels. Did they feel scared when they first started school?

- Now read the rest of Maya's story (pages 12–14). How does Maya feel now? If your children felt scared when they started school, how long did it take before they felt better?

- Read the first part of Jack's story (pages 15–17). Have your children ever got lost? Do they know someone who has been lost?

- Ask your children how they think Jack feels about being lost. Also ask them how Jack's dad might be feeling. Would he be just as scared as Jack? Why?

- Read the second part of Jack's story (pages 18–19). How do they think Jack feels now? How does Jack's dad feel? How does Maya feel?

- Look at pages 20–21 together. Then role-play comforting someone who is scared. Ask the children to take turns at being the person who is scared and the person who comforts them.